W9-CFG-272

DISNEY'S PIXAR®:

How Steve Jobs Changed Hollywood

WIZARDS OF TECHNOLOGY

WIZARDS OF TECHNOLOGY

DISNEY'S PIXAR®:

How Steve Jobs Changed Hollywood

AURELIA JACKSON

Mason Crest

Mason Crest
450 Parkway Drive, Suite D
Broomall, PA 19008
www.masoncrest.com

Printed and bound in the United States of America.

First printing
9 8 7 6 5 4 3 2 1

Series ISBN: 978-1-4222-3178-4
ISBN: 978-1-4222-3180-7
ebook ISBN: 978-1-4222-8716-3

Library of Congress Cataloging-in-Publication Data

Jackson, Aurelia.
  Disney's Pixar(tm) : how Steve Jobs changed Hollywood / Aurelia Jackson.
      pages cm. — (Wizards of technology)
   ISBN 978-1-4222-3180-7 (hardback) — ISBN 978-1-4222-3178-4 (series) — ISBN 978-1-4222-8716-3 (ebook) 1. Jobs, Steve, 1955-2011—Juvenile literature. 2. Pixar (Firm)—Juvenile literature. 3. Businesspeople—Biography—Juvenile literature. 4. Computer engineers—United States—Biography—Juvenile literature. 5. Animated films—United States—Juvenile literature. 6. Computer animation--United States—Juvenile literature. I. Title. II. Title: Disney's Pixar trademark. III. Title: Pixar.
  HD9696.2.U62J6355 2014
  338.7'614334092—dc23
                                        2014014807

CONTENTS

KEY ICONS TO LOOK FOR:

 Text-Dependent Questions: These questions send the reader back to the text for more careful attention to the evidence presented there.

 Words to Understand: These words with their easy-to-understand definitions will increase the reader's understanding of the text, while building vocabulary skills.

 Series Glossary of Key Terms: This back-of-the book glossary contains terminology used throughout this series. Words found here increase the reader's ability to read and comprehend higher-level books and articles in this field.

 Research Projects: Readers are pointed toward areas of further inquiry connected to each chapter. Suggestions are provided for projects that encourage deeper research and analysis.

 Sidebars: This boxed material within the main text allows readers to build knowledge, gain insights, explore possibilities, and broaden their perspectives by weaving together additional information to provide realistic and holistic perspectives.

Words to Understand

calligraphy: Decorative handwriting made with a pen or brush.

typography: The art of arranging typed text.

innovative: Done in a new and creative way.

humanistic: Having to do with the needs and feelings of people, instead of just focusing on technical things.

diverge: Go in two different directions.

CHAPTER ONE

The Man Who Made It All Possible

f you were to visit Pixar's headquarters, you'd find a pretty interesting place. The first thing you'd probably see when you walked in the door would be the giant plasma TV where the day's activities are listed— everything from live performances of Pixar films' soundtracks to aerobic exercise classes. The Smile Squad, guides wearing yellow T-shirts, would show you around. You'd see the Cereal Bar, where Pixar's staff can help themselves twenty-four hours a day to fourteen different kinds of breakfast cereal (most of them kids' cereals!) and an endless supply of milk. After the Cereal Bar, you might see the Pizza Room, where staff can grab a slice whenever they want. Then there's the Breathing Room, where people who need a break can go to sit quietly and meditate.

If you talked to some of the employees, you'd get an even better picture of what it's like to work at Pixar. Phil Shoebottom, for example, is a

The atrium of Pixar's headquarters shows the company's sense of fun and creativity—and also its success, as proven by the many awards visible in the display case.

technical director at Pixar. "I remember when I started, thinking it was the strangest place I'd ever seen," he told CNET. "One morning there was a half-naked guy standing on a table in the cafeteria, playing the saxophone. Or you'd leave to go to your car in the evening, and there'd be a ballroom dancing class in the atrium." Another technical director, Paul Oakley, told CNET, "There's something different every day. When we started working on *Monsters University*, everyone had to join a fraternity. My hazing process involved me dressing up as Mrs. Doubtfire for the day. I had to go to a director review in full makeup. But someone else was dressed as Tinky Winky from *Teletubbies*, so that was okay."

In general, you might think that the whole place seems a little like a thirteen-year-old's fantasy. But despite its fun and kooky workplace, Pixar is serious about what it does. The movies it makes show both sides of the company, both its goofiness and its commitment to excellence. It's been a winning combination for the company, and the twenty-six Academy Awards, five Golden Globes, and three Grammys that sit in a glass cabinet in Pixar's atrium are proof of that.

Back in 1985, though, Pixar was just a small, unsuccessful division of LucasFilms that was going nowhere. All that changed thanks to one man who turned the company into a brand-new kind of movie studio. In the years that followed, Pixar's computer-animated movies would become some of the most beloved films of all time—and the small company that had nearly disappeared would turn into a giant enterprise worth billions of dollars.

None of it would have happened without Steve Jobs.

Make Connections

Filmmaker George Lucas began LucasFilms back in 1971. The company became famous for blockbuster movies like *Star Wars* and *Indiana Jones*.

In 1982, Steve was on the cover of *Time* magazine.

STEVE'S EARLY LIFE

Steve Jobs was born in San Francisco on February 24, 1955. His biological parents were college graduate students who put him up for adoption when he was born. In 2005, Steve talked about his adoptive mother and why she wanted to adopt him.

> My biological mother was a young, unwed college graduate student, and she decided to put me up for adoption. She felt very strongly that I should be adopted by college graduates, so everything was all set for me to be adopted at birth by a lawyer and his wife. Except that when I popped out they decided at the last minute that they really wanted a girl. So my parents, who were on a waiting list, got a call in the middle of the night asking, "We have an unexpected baby boy; do you want him?" They said, "Of course."

Steve's birth mother was disappointed to learn that his new mother had never finished college, and his new father had never graduated from high school. Determined that her son would experience higher education, Steve's birth mother had second thoughts about the adoption.

"She refused to sign the final adoption papers," he said. "She only relented a few months later when my parents promised that I would someday go to college."

Paul and Clara Jobs of Mountain View, Santa Clara County, California, finally adopted Steve. Paul was a machinist, and Clara was an accountant. They raised Steve and saved money so they could one day send him to college, fulfilling their promise to their son's birth mother. In 1958, Steve got a little sister when his parents adopted a baby girl named Patti. (Years later, as an adult, Steve would also meet his birth sister Mona.)

Steve was a smart child, but he also had a hard time giving school his full attention. In the fourth grade, a teacher named Mrs. Hill gave Steve five-dollar bills and candy in order to get him to complete schoolwork and pay attention to class. Steve ended up doing so well in Mrs. Hill's class that he skipped fifth grade and moved into middle school. He attended Critten-den Middle School for a little while, before moving with his family to Los Altos, where he began attending Cupertino Junior High School.

As a student at Cupertino Junior High School and later at Homestead High School in Cupertino, Steve continued to show his intelligence, but he still had trouble focusing on school. Interested in computers and technology, he grew up learning from the engineers in his town; he also frequently attended after-school lectures at the Hewlett-Packard Company in Palo Alto, California. But Steve was also often in trouble for misbehaving; some of his pranks included releasing snakes in a classroom.

In 1972, Steve graduated from high school and prepared himself to move on to college. His parents were keeping their promise to Steve's birth mother by making sure he continued his education after high school.

STEVE AT COLLEGE

Steve enrolled in Reed College, a liberal arts school in Portland, Oregon. He didn't last long there, however. In fact, he dropped out after just one semester.

"I never graduated from college. Truth be told, this is the closest I've ever gotten to a college graduation," Steve said to graduating students during a commencement address at Stanford University in 2005.

> I dropped out of Reed College after the first six months . . . I couldn't see the value in it. I had no idea what I wanted to do with my life and no idea how college was going to help me figure it out. And here I was spending all of the money my parents had saved their entire life. So I decided to drop out and trust that it would all work out okay. It was pretty scary at the time, but looking back it was one of the best decisions I ever made. The minute I dropped out, I could stop taking the required classes that

didn't interest me, and begin dropping in on the ones that looked interesting.

Once he was free from the rigid structure of required courses, Steve began to really enjoy being a student. Now he could take classes that interested him, regardless of whether they fell into a specific degree program. Still, despite being happy with his decision, that period in his life came with some struggles.

"It wasn't all romantic," Steve told Stanford's class of 2005. "I didn't have a dorm room, so I slept on the floor in friends' rooms. I returned Coke bottles for the five-cent deposits to buy food with, and I would walk the seven miles across town every Sunday night to get one good meal a week at the Hare Krishna temple."

Despite those hardships, Steve was enjoying himself. "I loved it," he said. "And much of what I stumbled into by following my curiosity and intuition turned out to be priceless later on."

One of the classes Steve most enjoyed was **calligraphy**. The Reed College campus was covered with examples of this art, from posters to labels. Steve was fascinated by the creativity and decided to join the class to learn how to do it himself.

"I learned about serif and san-serif typefaces, about varying the amount of space between different letter combinations, about what makes great **typography** great," Steve told the graduating students of Stanford. "It was beautiful, historical, artistically subtle in a way that science can't capture, and I found it fascinating. None of this had even a hope of any practical application in my life."

Or so he thought. A decade later, when Steve and his friends were busily working to design the first Macintosh computer, he recalled this uncommon skill he'd picked up during his short time in college.

"We designed it all into the Mac. It was the first computer with beautiful typography," said Steve.

If I had never dropped in on that single course in college, the Mac would have never had multiple typefaces or proportionally spaced fonts. And since Windows just copied the Mac, it's likely that no personal computer would have them. If I had never dropped out, I would have never dropped in on this calligraphy class, and personal computers might not have the wonderful typography that they do.

That calligraphy class gave Steve one of the skills that would help him become one of the world's most *innovative* and creative minds of all time. "You can't connect the dots looking forward; you can only connect them looking backwards," he told the graduating class at Stanford. "So you have to trust that the dots will somehow connect in your future. You have to trust in something—your gut, destiny, life, karma, whatever. This approach has never let me down, and it has made all the difference in my life."

AFTER COLLEGE

In 1974, after leaving Reed College, Steve got a job working at Atari, one of the very first video game companies. Steve helped to create some of the era's most popular games while he worked at the company.

During this time, Steve was fascinated by the '70s' free-spirited atmosphere that was marked by the artistic brilliance of music legend Bob Dylan. "We'd drive huge distances to meet people who had . . . pictures or interviews with Bob Dylan," said Steve's good friend Steve Wozniak.

Steve met Wozniak when he was still in high school and the two remained friends through Steve's time at Reed College. Wozniak, known as "Woz," later went on to co-found Apple with Steve.

Steve was adventurous, and he wanted to see new things. He joined his friend, and future Apple employee, Daniel Kottke, on a backpacking trip to India and came back with a shaved head and a new perspective on life.

When Steve returned from India, he went back to working at Atari with his friend Steve Wozniak, designing video games. Woz was the stronger

The garage where it all began.

engineer, but Steve had creativity and business sense. The two designed and worked with computers as a hobby, becoming part of a group called the Homebrew Computer Club. Together, in 1976, they decided to create a new kind of computer.

STARTING APPLE

Before they could begin, however, the pair needed money. Steve sold his Volkswagen microbus for $1500, and Woz sold his prized Hewlett-Packard scientific calculator for $250. With enough money to start their new company, the two began working in the Jobs family garage, slowly beginning to build what would become an empire.

"I was lucky—I found what I loved to do early in life," Steve said. "Woz and I started Apple in my parents' garage when I was twenty." Steve told more of this story to the graduating class:

The early Apple computers looked a lot different from today's sleek laptops!

Make Connections

The name "Silicon Valley" was first used in 1971, when the name appeared in a magazine article called "Silicon Valley in the USA." The "valley" is the Santa Clara Valley near San Francisco. Silicon is a material used in computer parts. Many technology companies have been based in Silicon Valley at some point, and some of the biggest companies in the world were founded in the area. Silicon Valley is often thought of as the center of the technology, Internet, and computer industries in the United States and even the world.

Apple was this incredible journey. I mean we did some amazing things there. The thing that bound us together at Apple was the ability to make things that were going to change the world. That was very important. We were all pretty young. The average age in the company was mid-to-late twenties. Hardly anybody had families at the beginning and we all worked like maniacs and the greatest joy was that we felt we were fashioning collective works of art. . . . Something important that would last, that people contributed to and then could give to more people.

Apple's first employee was Steve's friend Daniel Kottke, who had joined Steve on his trip to India. All the young men involved in Apple's beginning, including Steve, were experienced in the use and creation of computers, but they also brought other passions to their work. "The Macintosh turned out so well because the people working on it were musicians, artists, poets, and historians who also happened to be excellent computer scientists," Steve said.

Steve Job's house in Palo Alto, California.

As the company continued to grow, Apple was soon on the forefront of innovation. By making computers smaller and more user-friendly, Apple paved the way for technologies and trends that have become so common-place that most people can't imagine life without them. Steve—and Apple as a whole—focused on creating technically sound products, while at the same time always making computers as easy to use as possible.

"The things I'm most proud about at Apple is where the technical and the **humanistic** came together," Steve said.

Although Apple was always pushing things forward and growing be-cause of its innovative products, Steve also said that Apple's rise to success was partly due to luck. He called Apple's early achievements a case of be-ing "at the right place at the right time."

Whether by luck, innovation, or the intelligence of its founders, Apple also succeeded in creating a new way of doing business. Most modern computer and software companies that have achieved success have done so by copying the model created by Apple.

Apple was making more money than any of the founders could have imagined. Steve was worth $200 million by the time he was twenty-five,

and he was on the cover of *Time* magazine the following year. The cover read, "Striking it rich, America's risk takers." Steve, with shaggy hair, mustache, and an apple on his head, was pictured next to an Apple computer.

But despite his important role in the creation and success of Apple, eventually Steve wasn't a good fit for the direction that Apple was heading. In 1985, he was fired from the company he had founded, and he decided it was time to move on.

"I've been thinking a lot and it's time for me to get on with my life," he said at an Apple board meeting. "It's obvious that I've got to do something. I'm thirty years old."

The stunning change was the result of internal turmoil that had been going on at Apple for years. "How can you get fired from a company you started?" he said, asking the question so many others were pondering at the time.

> Well, as Apple grew we hired someone who I thought was very talented to run the company with me, and for the first year or so things went well. But then our visions of the future began to **diverge** and eventually we had a falling out. When we did, our

Board of Directors sided with him. So at thirty I was out. And very publicly out. What had been the focus of my entire adult life was gone, and it was devastating.

When he left the company to which he'd devoted so much of himself, Steve felt lost. He thought about what he wanted his life to be, and what he'd done so far.

"I really didn't know what to do for a few months," he said. "I was a very public failure, and I even thought about running away from the [Silicon] Valley. But something slowly began to dawn on me—I still loved what I did. The turn of events at Apple had not changed that one bit. I had been rejected, but I was still in love. And so I decided to start over."

Disney · PIXAR

TOY STORY

Words to Understand

software: The programs that run on a computer.
CEO: Chief executive officer—the person in charge of running a company.
investors: People who put money into a company in the hopes that it will eventually earn more money back for them.
shares: Pieces of a company owned by people.

CHAPTER TWO

New Opportunities

Though Steve felt lost at first after leaving Apple, he still had his same passion for life—and the world still knew that he was truly a wizard of technology. President Reagan awarded the National Technology Medal to Steve in 1985 and the Jefferson Award for Public Service in 1987. Two years later, Steve was named Entrepreneur of the Decade by *Inc.* magazine.

Around the same time, Steve also fell in love with the woman who would become his wife, Laurene Powell. In March of 1991, the couple married, and that September, their first son, Reed, was born. "I didn't see

Ross Perot was one of the investors in Steve Job's company, NeXt. In 1992, Perot also ran—unsuccessfully—for president. The businessman had his finger in many pies!

it then, but it turned out that getting fired from Apple was the best thing that could have ever happened to me," Steve said later. "The heaviness of being successful was replaced by the lightness of being a beginner again, less sure about everything. It freed me to enter one of the most creative periods of my life."

During this period, Steve started a new company called NeXt, which he hoped to build into a competitor for Apple. The company was focused on *software* at first, but soon moved into making computers. Steve served as the company's *CEO*, and Texas businessman Ross Perot was one of NeXt's major *investors*.

Steve kept busy running NeXt—but a few earlier he had also taken chance on a different kind of business, a little company called Pixar. Steve decided to invest in the company. He also became its CEO.

THE BEGINNING OF PIXAR

When Steve first invested in the company, he was thinking he could turn it into a high-end computer hardware company. At the time, Pixar created a computer called the Pixar Image Computer, used by doctors and some parts of the government.

Sales weren't good, though. One of the company's employees, John Lasseter, decided to create some short animations that would show off the computer's capabilities. It didn't work out the way he'd hoped, though.

As poor sales threatened to put Pixar out of business, Steve invested more and more money in the company; after a few years, he owned it. Meanwhile, Lasseter's animation department was the only part of the company that had any success. His team began producing computer-animated commercials for companies like Tropicana, Listerine, and Life Savers.

In April 1990, Pixar sold its hardware division to Vicom Systems. All that was left now were the forty-two employees in Lasseter's animation

Pixar Image Computer, Pixar, US, 1986

In addition to movies generated entirely by computer, Pixar and Disney also jointly developed software allowing Pixar's Image Computer to color hand-drawn images for traditionally animated Disney cartoons.

The computer originally cost $135,000 and required an expensive workstation to operate it.

Speed: 11.8MHz Memory size: 100MB Memory type: Semiconductor Memory width: 32-bit Cost: $135,000

Gift of Loren Carpenter, 102671974

The clunky Pixar computer, sold mostly to government agencies and hospitals, was a long way from the movies for which the company would one day become famous!

department. They worked on commercials and a few short pieces for Nickelodeon and *Sesame Street*. Steve was wondering if he should sell the company, since it didn't seem to be going anywhere.

And then, in 1991, the little company had a stroke of luck—it made a $26 million deal with Disney to produce three computer-animated feature films, the first of which would be a movie called *Toy Story*.

During the next few years, despite its deal with Disney, the company was still losing money. Steve often thought about selling it. But as the years passed, and he watched *Toy Story* slowly take shape, he decided to give Pixar another chance.

TOY STORY

Steve was convinced that something amazing was being created. As scenes from the movie were finished, he watched them over and over. He invited his friends to come by his home to share his excitement. He was convinced that Pixar was on the brink of changing filmmaking forever.

Steve was right. When *Toy Story* came out in December 1995, it was an immediate success. No one had ever seen 3D animation like that in the movie—but it wasn't just the new technology that made the movie so magical. The story was carefully plotted, and the characters were lovable. People fell in love with Woody and the other toys.

Lasseter's team had worked hard to create each and every frame of the animation. Each frame lasts less than a second when you're watching the movie, but each of those frames has to be created separately. Some of them took as long as thirty hours to make. The artists and animators worked together hour after hour, making the animation move so smoothly that viewers believe the characters are "real." Lasseter said, "Every leaf and blade of grass had to be created. We had to give the world a sense of history. So the doors are banged up, the floors have scuffs."

Steve had bought Pixar because of its computer technology, but now he was totally won over by what Lasseter had accomplished. According to David Price, who wrote *The Pixar Touch*, Lasseter "wanted to build an

John Lasseter and his team of animators are the ones who brought to life Woody and Buzz Lightyear.

Make Connections

Making an animated film like *Toy Story* is a lot of work and takes a lot of people! Twenty-seven animators worked on the film, using 400 computer models to animate the characters. Each character was either created out of clay or was modeled from a computer-drawn diagram before reaching the computer animated design. Once the animators had a model for each character, the speech and movements were created, allowing each character to move in a variety of ways, such as talking, walking, or jumping. Of all of the characters, Woody was the hardest: he required 723 motion controls, including 212 for his face and 58 for his mouth. Every shot in the film eventually passed through the hands of eight different teams. To sync the characters' mouths and facial expressions to the actors' voices, animators spent a week per 8 seconds of animation. Next, the animators put the scenes together. They then added shading, lighting, and visual effects. Last of all, they used 300 computer processors to "render" the film to its final design, using computers that ran twenty-four hours a day. Rendering is the step where all the pieces are put together. Every three minutes of finished animation took about a week to render. In total, the film required 800,000 machine hours, countless human work hours, and 114,240 frames of animation.

animation studio, and it's a great tribute to Steve's genius that he was flexible enough to put aside his original idea of being a computer company owner with Pixar to turn it into the incredible artistic powerhouse it is."

With Apple, Steve had been the person with the know-how right from the beginning. It was his genius that made the company great. But with Pixar, Steve had a different role, even though he was the CEO. Steve wasn't an animator—but he did know how to make an environment where

Research Project

Find out more about computer animation, using the Internet and the library. What does it take to get a job in this field? What kind of education would you need? What would you need to be good at? How much would you get paid? Is this something that you might consider as a career? Why or why not?

Making Buzz Lightyear and all the other characters in *Toy Story* seem to run and talk took many, many hours of work.

Text-Dependent Questions

1. What did Pixar start out doing as a company?
2. Why did Steve consider selling Pixar?
3. Describe how an animated movie is made.
4. What was Steve Jobs' role at Pixar? How was it different from his role at Apple?

creativity could thrive. He understood that the best thing he could do for the company was to get out of the way of the creative people who were working so hard—and let them do what they loved.

Toy Story made more than $361 million worldwide. In 1996, Steve began to sell **shares** in Pixar to the public. The company's value steadily skyrocketed.

In the early days, Steve's money had kept the business afloat. Now, with a blockbuster film under its belt, Pixar was ready to become something truly amazing.

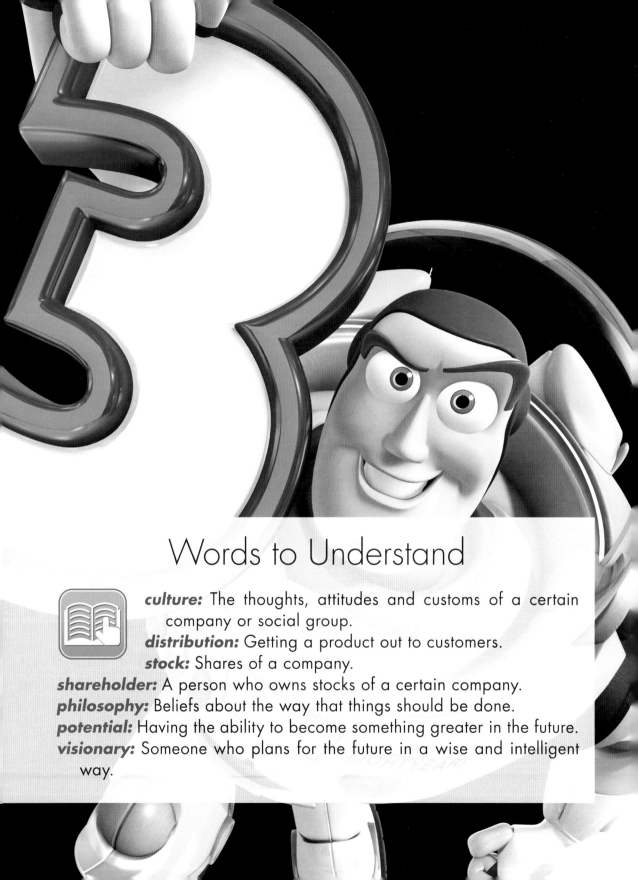

Words to Understand

culture: The thoughts, attitudes and customs of a certain company or social group.

distribution: Getting a product out to customers.

stock: Shares of a company.

shareholder: A person who owns stocks of a certain company.

philosophy: Beliefs about the way that things should be done.

potential: Having the ability to become something greater in the future.

visionary: Someone who plans for the future in a wise and intelligent way.

CHAPTER THREE

To Infinity and Beyond

With Pixar's new success, it was time for the company to move to a new building. Steve Jobs had definite ideas about how that building should be built. He knew he was never going to be the person who actually created Pixar's movies. But he could create a building where magic could happen.

First of all, he wanted there to be big central space in the building, where employees would have to bump into each other every day. The new building would have a huge two-story atrium where this could happen. In the center of the building would also be all the places to eat, as well as the only restrooms in the entire building. Steve believed the

After *Toy Story*'s success, Pixar built a new studio in Emeryville, California, which opened in November 2000.

building's structure would encourage a certain *culture* for his company, a culture where people would interact and bounce ideas off each other. He wanted to make an atmosphere that said, "Work is fun. Working hard means playing hard." The building would be not only a workplace but an enormous playground that would bring out each employees' sense of childlike wonder and playfulness.

Built around this central fun and magical place, each worker would have their own spaces. The employees could shape their own workspaces however they wanted. They strung colored lights, hung parachutes, and put up bunk beds. One person built a tiki hut as an office space; another created an Old West saloon. Each employee was encouraged to make his or her workspace a one-of-a-kind creative statement. Steve wanted to give the employees this opportunity as a way to build an environment of trust and respect. He wanted the building to say, "We're all creative and we're all in this together."

Steve was involved with every step of the building's construction. He picked the materials for the new building, right down to the door handles. He was convinced that this was the place where great movies would continue to be produced.

Steve was right. In the years that followed, Pixar created one award-winning film after another. Those movies were popular all around the world. People fell in love with Pixar's lovable Monsters, with Lightning McQueen and Nemo, with Wall•E and the Incredibles. Each movie was magic.

During these years that followed, Steve went back to Apple and picked up his responsibilities there. At Apple, he would again become a leader in the tech world. Meanwhile, he knew Pixar didn't need him in the same way. He spent about a day a week at the headquarters, where, according to David Price, his "major impact was on the strategic directions of the company. He had the crucial insight that Pixar would could one day be the equal of the Walt Disney Company in animation. He made this vision a reality."

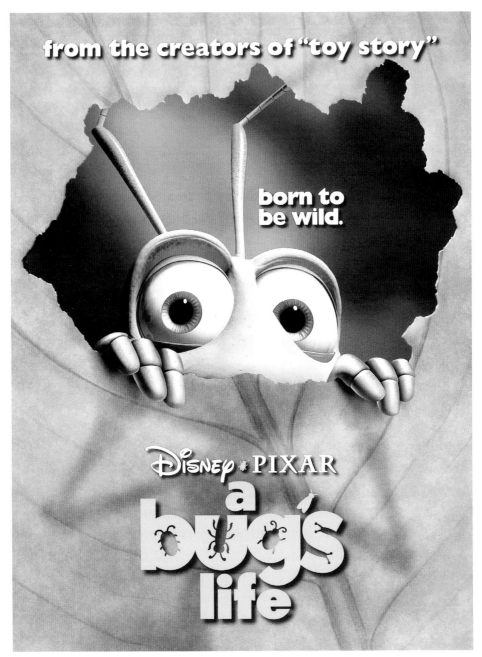

from the creators of "toy story"

born to
be wild.

Disney · PIXAR

a
bug's
life

Pixar's next film after *Toy Story* was *A Bug's Life*.

While Steve Jobs was still involved with Pixar, he went back to his old company, Apple—and revolutionized the world of telephone communications when he brought out the first iPhone.

Steve also knew that Disney wasn't only a competitor. He believed that if the two companies worked together, Pixar would be even stronger.

DISNEY AND PIXAR

After *Toy Story*'s release, Disney and Pixar argued over who had what rights. They knew that it would be good for both of them if they continued to work together—but they argued over the best way to do that.

Pixar wanted to control production and let Disney handle **distribution**, with Pixar collecting the profits and paying Disney a 10 or 15 percent

Disney's long history in animation and memorable characters made the large company a good fit for Pixar.

John Lasseter poses with *Ratatouille* writer and director Brad Bird at the movie's premier.

distribution fee. Once the movies were made, Steve wanted Pixar to also own the films. Disney didn't like these terms, but Steve held his ground and refused to give in.

Steve and Disney's CEO argued for years. Finally, in 2006, the two companies came to a new agreement. Disney would buy Pixar for $7.4 billion in Disney **stock**. This agreement made Steve Jobs the largest individual **shareholder** in Disney. He also had a seat now on Disney's board of directors.

As part of the deal, John Lasseter became the chief creative officer of both Pixar and Walt Disney Animation Studios. He also got the fun job of

Finding Nemo brought to life another cast of loveable characters.

being the principal creative adviser at Walt Disney Imagineering, which designs and builds the company's theme parks.

People on the outside worried that this merger would never work. They feared that the older, bigger company would squash Pixar's creative magic. But that didn't happen. Pixar continued to thrive.

Research Project

Use the library and the Internet to find out more about Walt Disney and the company he built. How did he get started? Describe the history of his company and the movies it made. In what ways was Walt Disney like Steve Jobs? How was he different?

A CREATIVE CULTURE

Pixar is like no other company. Each of its films is truly a product of its unique culture and *philosophy*.

Part of that philosophy is that mistakes are a necessary part of the creative process. Mistakes, says Pixar, are the only way creative works reach their full *potential*. John Lasseter once said, "Every Pixar film was, at one time or another, the worst motion picture ever made. People don't believe that, but it's true. But we don't give up on the films."

This philosophy apparently works. No other movie studio has had an unbroken run of blockbuster movies like Pixar has. Starting with the first *Toy Story*, followed by hit after hit, including *Cars*, *Ratatouille*, *Brave*, and *Toy Story 3*, Pixar's animation wizards proved that amazing, wonderful characters could be created in a whole new way. In the process, it made billions of dollars.

It wouldn't have happened without Steve Jobs. David Price sees Steve as the "accidental *visionary*" of the film industry. Steve created the atmosphere where Pixar's employees could do what they did best.

Steve never rushed a project. He insisted on waiting until something was good enough to be released. This gave John Lasseter and the other employees the space to make mistakes. It gave them time to make Pixar's films the absolute best they could be.

Movies like *Cars*, *Toy Story*, and *Finding Nemo* have made millions of dollars around the world, creating characters fans remember for years.

In an interview on PBS, Lasseter said that each of Pixar's movies contains the same themes that the company itself has: with the help of friends, we can overcome enormous obstacles and achieve amazing things. At the core of each movie, Lasseter said, "it's gotta be about the growth of the main character and how he changes."

That's Steve Job's story. And he made it Pixar's as well.

Newsweek

AMERICAN GENIUS

STEVE JOBS

HOW HE CHANGED OUR WORLD

Words to Understand

legacy: What you leave behind in the world.
intuition: A feeling about the way things are or how things should be done.

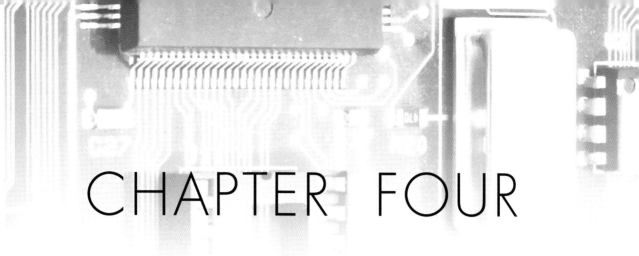

CHAPTER FOUR

Remembering Steve Jobs Today

n 2003, Steve's life suddenly changed. He had always taken good care of his health—but when he went to the doctor one day, a scan showed a tumor on his pancreas. His doctors told him it was most likely a type of cancer that could not be cured. He probably only had three to six months to live.

FACING DEATH

"I didn't even know what a pancreas was," Steve said later. "My doctor advised me to go home and get my affairs in order, which is doctor's code for prepare to die. It means to try to tell your kids everything you thought you'd have the next ten years to tell them in just a few months. It means to make sure everything is buttoned up so that it will be as easy as possible for your family. It means to say your goodbyes."

That's a very scary thing to be told. But it turned out that the tumor wasn't a death sentence after all, at least not yet. Steve had surgery at Stanford University Medical Center in Palo Alto, near his home—and afterward, he was given a clean bill of health.

"No one wants to die," Steve said. "Even people who want to go to heaven don't want to die to get there. And yet death is the destination we all share. No one has ever escaped it. And that is as it should be, because Death is very likely the single best invention of Life. It is Life's change agent. It clears out the old to make way for the new."

That first brush with cancer helped Steve take a clear, sharp look at his life. He valued each and every moment of it for the opportunities it had. But in some ways this approach to life was nothing new for him. For most of his life, he told the students at Stanford, "I have looked in the mirror every morning and asked myself, 'If today were the last day of my life, would I want to do what I am about to do today?' And whenever the answer has been 'No' for too many days in a row, I know I need to change something."

This was one of the secrets behind Steve's amazing life. He went on to say:

> Remembering that I'll be dead soon is the most important tool I've ever encountered to help me make the big choices in life. Because almost everything—all external expectations, all pride, all fear of embarrassment or failure—these things just fall away in the face of death, leaving only what is truly important. Remembering that you are going to die is the best way I know to avoid the trap of thinking you have something to lose. You are already naked. There is no reason not to follow your heart.

Make Connections

Your pancreas is deep inside you, sandwiched between your stomach and your spine. It produces juices that help break down the food you eat, so that your body can use it. Because of the pancreas' deep location, people often don't know they have cancer there until it grows large enough to get in the way of their other body organs, like the stomach and the liver.

As it turned out, Steve's cancer wasn't going to go away. It was going to cut short his amazing life. But he was going to leave behind a lasting *legacy*, something even bigger and better than iPods, MacBooks, *Toy Story*, or any of his other contributions. That was the example he set of what a person can do when he believes in his dreams and works hard to make them real.

"Your time is limited, so don't waste it living someone else's life," Steve told the graduating class at Stanford University. "Don't let the noise of others' opinions drown out your own inner voice. And most important, have the courage to follow your heart and *intuition*. They somehow already know what you truly want to become. Everything else is secondary."

STEVE'S DEATH

Steve battled cancer for years. All the while he continued working to make his companies the very best. During these years, Steve shared the iPhone and iPad with the world. Not even cancer could stop him from

Steve Job's willingness to do things differently brought amazing new things to the world.

Pixar has created a host of lovable characters who will live forever in the minds and hearts of everyone who has seen their movies.

giving the world more amazing new products that would change communication forever.

In August, 2011, Steve decided that even he couldn't keep working and fight his cancer. He told Apple fans and customers that he would be stepping down from the position he'd held two different times. "I have always said that if there ever came a day when I could no longer meet my duties and expectations as Apple's CEO, I would be the first to let you know," Steve wrote in a letter put out by Apple. "Unfortunately, that day has come."

People around the world left apples, Post-It notes with messages, and other tokens outside Apple Stores to express their grief at Steve's death.

Steve had survived many years longer than the three to six months that doctors first gave him. The ten years after he was first diagnosed with cancer had been filled with his usual hard work and amazing creativity. But in the end, death claimed him. In October of 2011, when Steve was fifty-six years old, he died of complications from his pancreatic cancer.

But even in his last days, he continued to be creative. Filled with tubes, unable to talk, he asked for a notepad and sketched out designs for a device that would hold an iPad in a hospital bed. He designed new hospital monitors and X-ray equipment.

Steve's sister Mona talked of his last moments. When she arrived at his Palo Alto home, she said, Steve and his wife Laurene "were talking and joking, and the kids were gathered around him." After a while, though, Steve fell silent. Then he looked off into the distance and said, "Oh WOW! Oh WOW! Oh WOW!"

Those were Steve Jobs' last words. They were a perfect expression of the way he lived his life, always searching for the beautiful, surprising, wondrous aspects of life.

Famous business and world leaders from around the globe expressed their sadness at Steve's death. Bill Gates, the founder of Apple rival Microsoft, wrote, "For those of us lucky enough to get to work with Steve, it's been an insanely great honor." He added, "I will miss Steve immensely." President Barack Obama issued this statement:

> Steve was among the greatest of American innovators—brave enough to think differently, bold enough to believe he could change the world, and talented enough to do it. . . . By making computers personal and putting the Internet in our pockets, he made the information revolution not only accessible, but intuitive and fun. And by turning his talents to storytelling, he has brought joy to millions of children and grownups alike. Steve was fond of saying that he lived every day like it was his last. Because he did, he transformed our lives, redefined entire industries, and

Toy Story is truly a part of our culture, as indicated by Woody and Jessie's faces on a U.S. postage stamp!

The Apple store in Shanghai, China. Steve's impact is still felt around the world today.

achieved one of the rarest feats in human history: he changed the way each of us sees the world.

"There is one more thing," Steve always said, right before he'd pull out some amazing new device. Now Apple fans knew that there would be no "one more thing" from Steve Jobs. The world had lost one of its brightest minds.

Steve had given the world so much, and now he was gone. Around the world, people considered how Apple's founder had changed their

Few businesspeople have had the effect that Steve had on the technology and culture of our time.

Research Project

Steve Jobs contributed many new things to the world, only a few of which have been mentioned in this book. Use the Internet and the library to find out more about all the amazing inventions Steve Jobs helped to create. Make a list of all the ways he changed our world, including music, computers, phones, and movies. He's been called the "Thomas Edison of our time." Explain why.

lives. Many people reacted as if they'd known him personally. For so many Apple fans, Steve was more than the leader of two great companies; he was a visionary and a leader. He was someone people looked up to. It was as if Steve had stepped into the future and brought back the best of what was to come each time he pulled another sleek Apple device from his pocket. The movies he had made possible had convinced people that computer-animated characters have hearts as big as any flesh-and-blood hero's.

STEVE'S LEGACY

The lives of just about everyone in America—and millions of people around the world—have been touched in some way by the creative endeavors of Steve Jobs. Whether it's someone listening to an iPod on their way to school, people using Apple computers to do their jobs, or families watching the latest exciting Pixar release, the impact that Steve had on modern culture is everywhere. Few people have done as much to shape the course of technology in the twenty-first century.

Steve had become one of America's most well-known billionaires, worth more than six billion dollars in 2010. He was named one of *Forbes*

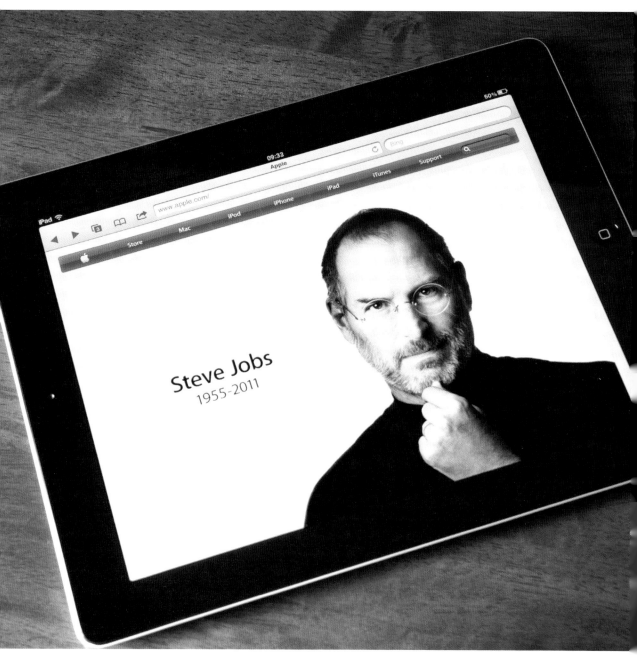

Steve Jobs will always be remembered for the ways he changed the world for the better.

magazine's World's Most Powerful People, *Fortune Magazine*'s CEO of the decade, and person of the year by *Time* magazine and the *Financial Times*. Few people ever achieve the kinds of success that Steve Jobs did in his life.

After John Lasseter heard about Steve's death, he said, "He saw the potential of what Pixar could be before the rest of us, and beyond what anyone ever imagined. Steve took a chance on us and believed in our crazy dream of making computer animated films; the one thing he always said was to simply 'make it great.' He is why Pixar turned out the way we did and his strength, integrity, and love of life has made us all better people. He will forever be a part of Pixar's DNA."

FIND OUT MORE

In Books

Beahm, George. *I, Steve: Steve Jobs in His Own Words*. Evanstown, IL: Agate, 2011.

Blumenthal, Karen. *Steve Jobs: The Man Who Thought Different*. New York: Square Fish, 2012.

Isaacson, Walter. *Steve Jobs*. New York: Simon and Schuster, 2011.

Paik, Karen. *To Infinity and Beyond! The Story of Pixar Animation Studios*. San Francisco, CA: Chronicle Books, 2007.

Price, David A. *The Pixar Touch*. New York: Vintage, 2008.

On the Internet

All About Steve Jobs
allaboutstevejobs.com

Apple: Remembering Steve Jobs
www.apple.com/stevejobs

How Pixar Fosters Collective Creativity
hbr.org/2008/09/how-pixar-fosters-collective-creativity

Pixar
www.pixar.com

Pixar Animation Studios
www.latimes.com/topic/economy-business-finance/media-industry/
movie-industry/pixar-animation-studios-ORCRP012232.topic

SERIES GLOSSARY
OF KEY TERMS

application: A program that runs on a computer or smartphone. People often call these "apps."

bug: A problem with how a program runs.

byte: A unit of information stored on a computer. One byte is equal to eight digits of binary code—that's eight 1s or 0s.

cloud: Data and apps that are stored on the Internet instead of on your own computer or smartphone are said to be "in the cloud."

data: Information stored on a computer.

debug: Find the problems with an app or program and fix them.

device: Your computer, smartphone, or other piece of technology. Devices can often access the Internet and run apps.

digital: Having to do with computers or stored on a computer.

hardware: The physical part of a computer. The hardware is made up of the parts you can see and touch.

memory: Somewhere that a computer stores information that it is using.

media: Short for multimedia, it's the entertainment or information that can be stored on a computer. Examples of media include music, videos, and e-books.

network: More than one computer or device connected together so information can be shared between them.

pixel: A dot of light or color on a digital display. A computer monitor or phone screen has lots of pixels that work together to create an image.

program: A collection of computer code that does a job.

software: Programs that run on a computer.

technology: Something that people invent to make a job easier or do something new.

INDEX

ABOUT THE AUTHOR

Aurelia Jackson is a writer living and working in New York City. She has a passion for writing and a love of education, both of which she brings to all the work she does.

PICTURE CREDITS